This Journal For:

_____

_____

_____

_____

My Life Stories

My Past Lessons For You and Notes

My Life Stories

My Past Lessons For You and Notes

My Life Stories

My Past Lessons For You and Notes

My Life Stories

My Past Lessons For You and Notes

My Life Stories

My Past Lessons For You and Notes

My Life Stories

My Past Lessons For You and Notes

My Life Stories

My Past Lessons For You and Notes

My Life Stories

My Past Lessons For You and Notes

My Life Stories

My Past Lessons For You and Notes

My Life Stories

My Past Lessons For You and Notes

My Life Stories

My Past Lessons For You and Notes

My Life Stories

My Past Lessons For You and Notes

My Life Stories

My Past Lessons For You and Notes

My Life Stories

My Past Lessons For You and Notes

My Life Stories

My Past Lessons For You and Notes

My Life Stories

My Past Lessons For You and Notes

My Life Stories

My Past Lessons For You and Notes

My Life Stories

My Past Lessons For You and Notes

My Life Stories

My Past Lessons For You and Notes

My Life Stories

My Past Lessons For You and Notes

My Life Stories

My Past Lessons For You and Notes

My Life Stories

My Past Lessons For You and Notes

My Life Stories

My Past Lessons For You and Notes

My Life Stories

My Past Lessons For You and Notes

My Life Stories

My Past Lessons For You and Notes

My Life Stories

My Past Lessons For You and Notes

My Life Stories

My Past Lessons For You and Notes

My Life Stories

My Past Lessons For You and Notes

My Life Stories

My Past Lessons For You and Notes

My Life Stories

My Past Lessons For You and Notes

My Life Stories

My Past Lessons For You and Notes

My Life Stories

My Past Lessons For You and Notes

My Life Stories

My Past Lessons For You and Notes

My Life Stories

My Past Lessons For You and Notes

My Life Stories

My Past Lessons For You and Notes

My Life Stories

My Past Lessons For You and Notes

My Life Stories

My Past Lessons For You and Notes

My Life Stories

My Past Lessons For You and Notes

My Life Stories

My Past Lessons For You and Notes

My Life Stories

My Past Lessons For You and Notes

My Life Stories

My Past Lessons For You and Notes

My Life Stories

My Past Lessons For You and Notes

My Life Stories

My Past Lessons For You and Notes

My Life Stories

My Past Lessons For You and Notes

My Life Stories

My Past Lessons For You and Notes

My Life Stories

My Past Lessons For You and Notes

My Life Stories

My Past Lessons For You and Notes

My Life Stories

My Past Lessons For You and Notes

My Life Stories

My Past Lessons For You and Notes

My Life Stories

My Past Lessons For You and Notes

My Life Stories

My Past Lessons For You and Notes

My Life Stories

My Past Lessons For You and Notes

My Life Stories

My Past Lessons For You and Notes

My Life Stories

My Past Lessons For You and Notes

My Life Stories

My Past Lessons For You and Notes

My Life Stories

My Past Lessons For You and Notes

My Life Stories

My Past Lessons For You and Notes

My Life Stories

My Past Lessons For You and Notes

My Life Stories

My Past Lessons For You and Notes

Made in United States
Orlando, FL
08 April 2023